Grumb...

by M...

Illustrations by Peter Lole

RAINBOW READING

"I want to go home," grumbled Kim.
"I hate it at this park. I hate these ugly white shoes and I hate those silly ducks swimming round and round."

She kicked out at the ducks and her new white shoe came off her foot and flew high into the air.
It bounced off a duck's back, then it splashed into the lake.

"That was a stupid thing to do,"
growled her Mum.
"Those shoes are brand new and they cost a lot of money. And there was no need to kick out at the poor ducks."
"I didn't mean to hit a duck and I didn't mean for my shoe to come off," said Kim.
"Go and ask the man doing the garden if we can borrow his rake," said Dad.

Dad raked and raked the bottom of the lake where the shoe had landed. He raked up a drink can and a red shoe.
Then he raked a little to the left and up came some lolly wrappers and a white hat, but no white shoe.

Mum raked and raked the bottom of the lake where the shoe had landed. She raked up a drink bottle and a brown shoe.
Then she raked a little to the right and up came a pie bag and an iceblock stick, but no white shoe.

"It's lost," said Mum. "Let's go home. Go and get in the car."

"I don't want to go home yet," grumbled Kim. "I love it at this park. I want to find my favourite shoe and I want to watch those cute ducks swimming round and round."